Because

Brian Hugged His Mother

By David L. Rice   Illustrated by K. Dyble Thompson

Dawn Publications

Dedication

To Steven's, Brian's and Joanna's mother
—who taught them to hug! —DR

To Father and Mother. —KDT

Library of Congress Cataloging-in-Publication Data

Rice, David L., 1939-
        Because Brian hugged his mother / by David L. Rice ; illus-trated by K. Dyble Thompson.
        p.cm.
        Summary: When Brian hugs and kisses his mother one morning, the act starts a chain reaction of kindness and consider-ation that spreads throughout the town and eventually comes back to him.
        ISBN 1-883220-90-4 (hardcover). ISBN 1-883220-89-0 (pbk.)
        [1. Kindness—Fiction. 2. Conduct of life—Fiction. 3. City and town life—Fiction.] I. Thompson, Kathryn Dyble, ill. II. Title.
PZ7.R36185Be 1999
[Fic]—dc21   98-46381
                                                                        CIP
                                                                        AC

Dawn Publications
12402 Bitney Springs Rd
Nevada City, CA 95959
800-545-7475
Email: nature@DawnPub.com
Website: www.DawnPub.com

Printed in China

10 9 8 7 6 5 4
First Edition

Computer production by Rob Froelick

Be kind in all you say and do,

'Cause acts of kindness follow you:

With just one kindness a chain will start

To grow and glow from heart to heart!

Brian woke up feeling great! He ran into the kitchen, and gave his mother a kiss and a great big hug.

"I love you, Mom! You're the best mom in the whole world!"

Brian's mother felt loved and appreciated.

Because Brian's mother was feeling loved and appreciated, she made Brian and his sister, Joanna, their favorite breakfast of waffles with peanut butter and whipped cream on top.

"I'm so glad you're my children. You bring me so much happiness."

Brian and Joanna felt loved and cherished.

Because Joanna was feeling loved and cherished, she helped her teacher, Mr. Emerson, get the classroom ready for school.

"I like helping you, Mr. Emerson. You're a good teacher. You make learning fun."

Mr. Emerson felt competent and successful.

Because Mr. Emerson was feeling competent and successful, he had the class make Ms. Sanchez, the new principal, a banner for her birthday.

"Happy Birthday, Ms. Sanchez. We're really glad you came to our school."

Ms. Sanchez felt wanted and accepted.

DAY

Because Ms. Sanchez was feeling wanted and accepted, she was especially patient with Lorreta, who had been sent to the office for bringing a jar of her dog's fleas to school and accidentally letting them go.

"It's O.K., Lorreta. Next time, ask your teacher before bringing insects to school, even if they are your pets."

Lorreta felt understood ... and a little bit itchy!

Because Lorreta was feeling
understood, she didn't tease
Richard when she noticed his
pants were unzipped. Instead, she
whispered in his ear as she passed
him, "X Y Z," which, of course,
means "examine your zipper."
Richard rushed into the bathroom to
zip up. He felt relieved that Lorreta
hadn't teased him or told the other girls.

Richard was still feeling relieved when he saw his little brother Eddie, who was in kindergarten, waiting for the bus. Richard didn't mention that Eddie's shoes were on the wrong feet and his shirt was buttoned lopsided.

"I really like your picture, Eddie. You did a great job."

Eddie felt proud and grown up.

Because Eddie was feeling proud and grown up, he gave Ms. Wong, his bus driver, the picture he had painted.

"This is for you, Ms. Wong. You always say hello to me and don't get upset when I'm a little late."

Ms. Wong felt respected and appreciated.

Because Ms. Wong was feeling respected and appreciated, she let a large truck, that had been waiting in traffic for a long time, get in front of her bus. The truck driver smiled and waved.

Because the truck driver was feeling thankful, he helped the stock clerk at the market unload the truck.

"You look like you've had a long day. Let me help you unload."

The stock clerk felt grateful and encouraged.

Because the stock clerk was feeling grateful and encouraged, he gave Mrs. Johnson some free cans of dog food when she picked up a special order of cheese-covered mouse tails for her cat Tiffany.

"These cans have dents but they're still good. We appreciate your shopping here. You're one of our friendliest customers."

Mrs. Johnson felt valued.

Because Mrs. Johnson was feeling valued, she let her dog, Jumbo, watch his favorite video, Super Dog, when she got home.

"Have a good time, Jumbo. But don't bark too loud—last time the neighbors complained."

Jumbo felt excited and happy.

Because Jumbo was happily watching his video, he didn't tease Tiffany when she came in to lie by the fire.

Tiffany felt content and peaceful as she relaxed by the fire.

Because Tiffany was feeling content and peaceful, she jumped up on Mrs. Gunderson's lap when she came to visit.

"Just listen to her purr. Tiffany seems unusually friendly today. Sometimes she doesn't even let me pet her."

Mrs. Gunderson felt pleased and accepted.

Because Mrs. Gunderson was feeling pleased and accepted, she was understanding when her mechanic called with bad news about her car.

"I was hoping I wouldn't have to replace the brakes, but if you say they need it, I know they do."

The mechanic felt respected and trusted.

Because the mechanic was feeling respected and trusted, he remembered to thank the mail carrier when he delivered the mail.

"I can't thank you enough for leaving that package next door yesterday when I wasn't here. If I hadn't had that car part, I might have lost a good customer. You're the best mail carrier we've ever had."

The mail carrier felt efficient and capable.

Because the mail carrier was feeling efficient and capable, he remembered to compliment the baker when he delivered her mail.

"That cake you made for my daughter's birthday was delicious. Everyone just loved how you made it in the shape of a drum set."

The baker felt talented and artistic.

Because the baker was feeling talented and artistic, she took her dentist some tasty carrot and raisin bran muffins when she went for her checkup.

"I really appreciate the great job you do keeping my teeth and gums healthy and looking nice."

Her dentist felt valued and professional.

Because the dentist was feeling valued and professional, she told the chef at the restaurant how good her dinner had been.

"That was the best split pea and lima bean soup I have ever had. You are such a treasure. I'm so glad I discovered your restaurant."

The chef felt masterful and creative.

Because the chef was feeling masterful and creative, he fixed Officer Williamson her favorite meal of eggplant, zucchini, and cauliflower, when she came in on her dinner break.

"I also made your favorite dessert. It's my way of saying thank you for keeping our city safe."

Officer Williamson felt supported and honored.

Because Officer Williamson was feeling supported and honored, she didn't give Brian's father a ticket when she stopped him for speeding.

"I'll just give you a warning this time. But you should slow down or you're going to have an accident."

Brian's father felt grateful and relieved.

Because Brian's father was feeling grateful and relieved, he only gave Brian's older brother, Steve, a warning when he saw him riding his skateboard in the street.

"If you ride in the street again, you'll lose your skateboard for a week. I'm really worried that you might get hit by a car."

Later that evening, Brian's dad took an extra long time alone with Brian. They read two books and talked about the day.

"It's so great to have you as my son. You're such an important part of my life," his father said, giving Brian a long hug.

Brian felt loved and treasured.

Because Brian went to sleep feeling loved and treasured, he had pleasant dreams and slept wonderfully. When he woke up the next morning, he felt great! He ran into the kitchen and he—well, you know what he did.

David L. Rice learned random acts of kindness from his parents, who were always ready to help someone in need. The Golden Rule was taught by example, not just words. One of his top priorities as a teacher and parent has been to promote the understanding that treating others kindly results in feeling better about ourselves and having happier lives. He discusses this and other important values during his visits to schools across the country. His first book, *Lifetimes,* also published by Dawn Publications, emphasizes the importance of all of Nature's creations.

K. Dyble Thompson enjoys watching people of all kinds—young and old, working and at play. In her art, she loves to play with puns and show silly scenarios. She has a degree in fine arts from the University of Wisconsin at Milwaukee. In addition to her book illustrations, she is known as a muralist and a pavement artist.

OTHER DISTINCTIVE NATURE AWARENESS BOOKS FROM DAWN PUBLICATIONS

Lifetimes, also by David Rice, introduces some of nature's longest, shortest, and most unusual lifetimes, and what they have to teach us. This book teaches, but it also goes right to the heart. (Teacher's Guide available.)

Do Animals Have Feeling, Too? also by David Rice, presents fascinating true stories of animal behavior, and then asks the reader whether they think the animal is acting on the basis of feelings or just instinctively.

Stickeen, John Muir and the Brave Little Dog, by John Muir as retold by Donnell Rubay. Surrounded by deep canyons of ice, John Muir and a little black dog wonder: are they doomed? How they handle the challenge, and are changed by it, creates a classic story—"the most memorable of all my wild days," as Muir later wrote of this 1880 adventure in Alaska.

Wonderful Nature, Wonderful You, by Karin Ireland, shows how nature is a great teacher, reminding us to bloom where we are planted. Qualities of nature become a metaphor for positive values and self-esteem. Illustrated by Christopher Canyon.

Motherlove, by Virginia Kroll. The love of a mother for her young, it is said, is the best echo of love divine. In animal and the human species alike, a mother's love gives and forgives, directs and protects and puts the heart in a home. This book is a celebration of motherlove.

The Sharing Nature With Children Series of Teacher's Guides is distinctive in that they integrate character education with core science and language arts curricula.

Dawn Publications is dedicated to inspiring in children a deeper understanding and appreciation for all life on Earth. To order, or for a copy of our catalog, please call 800-545-7475. Please also visit our web site at www.DawnPub.com.